THE GREATEST STORY EVER TOLD

by

____

(Your Name)

Inspired by

JOHN C. MAXWELL

CENTER STREET

NASHVILLE NEW YORK

Dear Friend,

The Greatest Story Ever Told can only be written by you. I want you to fill these blank pages with intentional acts of kindness that add value to people. Everyday let your words be a record of how you are making a positive difference in the lives of others. Start now & intentionally make a great story with your life.

Your friend

John C. Maxwell

Please Share Your Story with Us and Others

As you fill these pages, start sharing your story. If you need help with how to summarize it so that you can share it with others, you can do so by answering each of the following questions. Use a paragraph for each answer. Together, the paragraphs will tell a version of your story.

1. **Reality:** What were you like before you became intentional about making a difference and being proactive about "writing" your life story?
2. **Discovery:** What did you learn that made you want to change? If there was a specific moment of discovery or an incident that impacted you, please write about it.
3. **Change:** What are the most important changes you have made?
4. **Results:** How have those changes helped you?
5. **Sharing:** What lesson would you like others to know from your experience?
6. **Significance:** How do you hope the lesson you learned will help the person reading your story?

If you want to become one of the million people inspired by John Maxwell to tell their stories of intentional living, please go to MyIntentionalLivingStory.com. Tell about your experience so that you can inspire others.

John C. Maxwell and The John Maxwell Leadership Foundation are represented by Yates & Yates, www.yates2.com.

Center Street
Hachette Book Group
1290 Avenue of the Americas
New York, NY 10104
centerstreet.com
twitter.com/centerstreet

First Edition: November 2016

Center Street is a division of Hachette Book Group, Inc.
The Center Street name and logo are trademarks of
Hachette Book Group, Inc.

ISBN: 978-1-4555-6958-8

Printed in the United States of America

LSC-C

10 9 8 7 6 5 4 3 2